# LIGHTING THE SHADOWS

DONAL NEARY SJ

# LIGHTING THE SHADOWS

## Prayers and Reflections for Young People

VERITAS

First published 1995 by
Veritas Publications
7/8 Lower Abbey Street
Dublin 1



ISBN 1 85390 228 4

Cover photograph by The Telegraph
Cover design by Banahan McManus Ltd, Dublin
Printed in the Republic of Ireland by Criterion Press Ltd, Dublin

# CONTENTS

# INTRODUCTION

*Lighting the Shadows* invites you to pray from your own experience, from the world you live in, and from some of the words of Jesus in the gospel. Following on *The Calm Beneath the Storm*, it will prove particularly helpful to the 15-25 age group, and others also.

The prayers of *Lighting the Shadows* will start you praying. There are many experiences which might spur you to some prayer – experiences of life for which you are grateful, ways in which you struggle – and you may find some of your own favourite Scripture.

As you pray these prayers, pause when you wish and continue in your own words. For example, the prayer 'Secrets' gives space for you to mention your own particular secrets to God. Other prayers will lend themselves to your own personal words. You may even write some of your own prayers from these.

The experiences of another can help you pray from a similar experience of your own, or one that was like the author's. For example, in the prayer 'A stutter' you may find yourself praying about similar reactions to a different experience. For one person the problem was his stutter, for another it might be a scar, or limp.

The words of another also can help you to pray when you cannot find words yourself, and introduce you to a way of praying. They never 'do' the praying for you. I hope these prayers will bring you in touch with God who is close to you, for Jesus says that 'We make our home in you'. The closest you will find God is in your own experience: your struggles, your hopes, joys, griefs, darknesses and brightnesses. In all of the shadows of life is found the light of God in the risen Lord Jesus.

The prayers of *Lighting the Shadows* may also be used for reflections at liturgy and prayer meetings, and may be easily adapted to different circumstances and age groups.

These prayers come out of many people's experiences. Some are personal to me, others I have been privileged to hear on retreats and in friendship with a large number of people. To these I am very grateful for the enrichment I have received, and I know that I am only their 'pen' to share their lives and their faith in this book.

Donal Neary SJ
January 1995

## *1* Be not afraid

In the fears of my life, Lord, be near.

When I lose a friendship and love seems far distant,
and I fear I'll never find love again,
or I fail in an exam
and I fear that my results can never improve,
or I don't get a job,
and I fear I'll never be employed,

be near me, Lord,
be near and touch me with your confidence.
If I feel I'll lose my parents' love
or that they'll not make up their differences,
or when I'm left last at home and I feel so lonely,
or when someone close is very ill or dies,
and I fear the future can be so fragile,
be near, Lord God, and give me hope.

If I fear death or illness,
failure or loneliness,
in all the fear I have,
please, Lord, let me know you,
the One who is always near,
friend and guide on the journey.

When I've lost my something dear,
help me to admit my disappointment and anger,
or guilt or sadness or regrets.

Help me to love even when I'm hurt,
and even, slowly, to forgive.

Let me not carry my fears through the future like a
heavy burden,
but put fear, where it best belongs, into your hands.
Help me to value what is good in all my experiences,
even when it's loss and pain and fear.

Let me hear in my heart your words,
'It is I; do not be afraid.'

Let these words echo within my losses and fears.
Let these words be the echo inside me
of your peace, your strength,
your guidance
and your love.

Replace my fear with trust in you,
for you have said,
'It is I; do not be afraid.'

## *2* I FORGIVE YOU

Often, Lord, I feel dirty inside.
I don't tell anyone about it,
but I want to be forgiven.
Maybe for gossip, or lies,
and I know I didn't mean to talk like that;
or jealousy bringing on harsh attitudes to people,

or ways I use people just for prestige, pleasure or money,
with little respect for their feelings.

I looked across the class yesterday,
and I know the way he looked at me
that he knew I didn't really care for him.
I just wanted to be seen with him,
some closeness just for a while,
using him, and he was maybe using me;
I feel sorry, a bit unclean on the inside,
it was a show of love and not sincere.

You said to people in the gospel,
'Your sins are forgiven,
I don't condemn you';
you seemed to spread forgiveness about you
like an embrace, a hug
or a warm, strong handshake.

Forgive me, and more,
let me know I am forgiven.

I don't want to use people like I do.
Can you help me?

Let me know that you love me, forgive me,
and that you are the same to others.
This might help me forgive myself and
be kinder in the ways I think and speak about others.

Thanks, Lord, for your forgiveness.

## 3 Come, follow me

Now and then, Lord, these words haunt me.
Other times they seem very loud in my ears,
and I get a buzz from them.

Help me hear them well.

I have decisions to make about my life,
and at times I get stuck about them.
It's like a lot of voices at the same time,
or a radio with different stations crackling over each other.

Come, follow money,
come, follow prestige,
come, follow friends,
come, follow power.

Then, your voice, Lord,
maybe in a gospel I hear at Mass,
or in someone I met who has followed you,
or in the poverty all around the world.
Can I answer?

Give me the courage to ask the question of myself,
Lord,
when I'm confused and out of sorts;
courage to ask what my heart is saying to me
when I'm feeling generous and at peace.
Lord, I want to follow you
and I don't know how.
And help me to know, Lord, that
there is happiness in following you.
Help me to be a follower of you,
in a job, in marriage,
in single life, in religious life,
in priesthood, in voluntary service,
however the path may lead.
In whatever way I can bring the gospel to life,
and live my life out of love,
then I am following you.

Lord, I trust that your hand is reaching out for me
when I want to let your words,
come, follow me,
enter deeply into my decisions.

Your words open the path of life for me;
they give me a wide vision of life,
a meaning in my heart
that will last forever,
and will be at the centre of other decisions
I'll make later.

## *4* You are my friends

That's what You call each of us, Lord,
Your name for us on the night before You died.
Thanks for Your friendship.

There are times, Lord, when I feel so bad in myself,
that I can't believe You'd call me a friend.
Things happen that make me feel inferior –
what people say about me,
or dishonesty I've got into,
when someone likes me only for my money,
or my body, or my other friends,
and then I feel I'm not much good myself.

Help me then, Lord, to hear the words,
'You are my friends',
and know that I'm right in the middle of
Your circle of friends.

That's when I get confused
and feel ashamed of who I am,
or guilty in myself
for experiences I've got into.

And then the times when I feel alive,
and that I am okay, good in myself.
Others may let me know that sometimes,
other times I feel it in myself,
like a drink of joy inside me.
I know then also
that You are near,
a faithful friend.

And then, when I know You are always a friend,
I can feel better about myself
and know I'm okay in Your eyes.

I need someone, Lord,
who is always there;
friends and family are like that sometimes,
but You're different.

Is Your promise true,
that You will always call me a friend?
Help me believe that, Lord,
and help me return friendship to You.
And if You say this to me,
'You are my friends',
You are saying it to everyone.

Lord, take me into the circle of Your friendship,
and let me believe I belong there,
in the way I welcome Your friendship
and live by Your word and values.
Thanks for being a friend.

## *5* Strengthen me, Lord

Strengthen me, Lord,
heal me,
forgive me.

There's the pain of the past that needs healing:

let down by another
which made trusting difficult,
or made intimacy painful,
and I know I need healing.

Lord, fill the past with confidence,
with the assurance that nothing of the past
need be a lifelong wound or burden.
Fill the unloved places of my heart with Your love;
those places of my heart which hold the people who
hurt me,
which contain the failures that keep me down
and which enfold the hatreds of my heart.

And forgive me, Lord;
those painful past memories
of people I hurt, friends I let down,
relationships needlessly neglected,
abuse of another's love,
neglect of You.
Draw that curtain of blame back
so that I can be warmed by Your forgiveness.

And strengthen me;
I want to love,
to be generous, to be idealistic.
And then I just fail and fall;
hurts take over and I draw back from helping,
my confidence flags and I'm afraid to reach out to another;
my heart grows fearful and I don't have the courage to
pray.

Within each of us
there are empty places,
like an empty pool or pond
waiting for living water;
like a ship in the fog,
looking for direction,
or a note waiting for harmony.

*What is an emptiness for you? Your failures, disappointments, sins?*

*Talk to the Lord about them. Tell him how you feel.*

Lord, speak Your word to me,
like You spoke to men and women
who came to You
for strength,
for healing,
for forgiveness.

To a woman who felt wretched about herself
after being found committing adultery,
Jesus said, 'I do not condemn you';

to the woman who met him at the roadside
when she came for water and to put together
a shattered life of battered relationships,
he said, 'Ask and I will give you living water'.

And to everyone he says about his Father and himself,
'We will make our home in you'.

*Echo these words of Jesus in your mind as they fit; repeat them, even one of them.*

Heal me, Lord,
strengthen me, forgive me,
in the secret soul-places which
need, want, yearn, cry out for
Your healing,
Your strength,
Your forgiveness.

## *6* You are near

Thank You, Lord.
I can recognise you
in the beauty of nature,
the smile of a child,
the sympathy of a friend.
That's how I can see Your face,
hear Your voice,
feel Your hand,
sense Your presence.

Thank You, Lord.
In the simple goodness of the family,
the phone call from someone away,
the visit, the letter, a prayer,
the ways people look after and care for each other,
I can recognise
Your help, concern and care for us.

In all the questions I have about You,
like Your attitude to people's sufferings,
like what You are really like,
like whether You are close or far away from us,
help me to recognise the simple things
that are real signs that You are near.

Thank You, Lord.

## 7 Away for the summer

I wonder how they are, Lord.
My brother and sister are away
looking for summer work.
We really miss them.
The house is very quiet without them
and the two of us feel a bit left behind.
We talk about them a lot,
and I know Mum and Dad worry about them.
Keep them safe from danger,
help them get jobs.
Don't let them be used in any way.
Let them enjoy the months away from home
and make new friends.
I hope they don't forget us,
and it's great to get a letter or a phone call,
even though it's hard to know what to say on the
phone.

Thanks for the contact, Lord,
and it's good to miss them
because then we know we love them.
Look after them, Lord;
let them know we care for them,
and we trust them to You, Lord;
You love them more than even we do.

## 8 Away from home

It's great to be away in a new place, Lord.
I enjoy new people, a new job, a new country.
I'm grateful for the opportunity to travel.

But I miss them at home, some times more than others.
I hope they're okay.
Look after them.
I know they miss me,
but they're glad of my new opportunities.

Sometimes it's strange and lonely;
I'm like a car driving on the wrong side of the road,
or a child in a room not knowing what to say.
Or a fear that I'll run out of money,
or the job will fold up.
Other times I dread going home again;
will I have changed a lot?

Lord, help me to see the good things of home,
the people whose friendship I value,
the family who love me.

Help me nourish my roots
with new experiences.
Help me value home more
by being somewhere new.
And let me find You, Lord,
friend at home and away.

## *9* Illness

Lord, look after...
You know he's sick and he's very worried;
due to go for a big operation tomorrow.

I'm just praying for him.
I don't know what to say.
You love him, so You're on his side.

Make him better;
give him health,
for his own sake and his wife's
and the children he loves and who love him,
and in all the fears they have,
give him, and them,
peace of body, mind and spirit,
and hope in Your love,
no matter what the outcome.
Give him peace for himself;
he's worried and anxious
and puts on a brave face.
Let him believe
that so many have gone through this operation
and it has been successful
and they are well now.
Give him trust as well as peace;
trust that nothing happens in life outside Your love.

It's hard to trust in You, Lord,
when we're in trouble and in pain.

Hard to believe You really care.
But then sometimes in the middle of all the confusion
I realise that You are near,
closer to me than the dawn to the light,
than the tide to the water,
than the leaf to its colour.

I believe this, Lord,
help him to believe it also.

All I can say Lord, is the gospel prayer,
'he whom You love is sick.'

Make him better, Lord;
give him courage and peace,
in body, mind and soul,
and give the same to the people close to him.

In all our illnesses, Lord,
bring us closer to You,
help us know You are with us,
in life, in death,
in illness and in health.

## *10* Bullying

I saw his frustration, Lord,
as he was bullied again.
He's just a bit smaller than the rest of us,
and seems to bring out the bully in us.

I'd love to take his part but I'm afraid.

I can see girls laughing when it's happening,
but you can see the hurt in their eyes for him.
There's a tear in my heart for him.
The mockery is like a crown of thorns on his head –
he must dread coming to school.

Why do we pick on weaknesses in people, Lord?
I know I have laughed at him sometimes,
and I hate it when people laugh at my height.
I know I'm tall, but that doesn't make me a freak.

I just pray for him now, Lord.
I pray he won't be too damaged,
and I pray that I'll do something about it,
either stand up for him,
be friendly to him
or talk to a teacher about it.

Help us, Lord, to build up the good in each other,
not laugh at the weaknesses.
Some day the bullies will be left alone,
because nobody puts up with loud mouths forever.
Help them see the light also, Lord,
and give up making life hell for a gentle person.

Give me the courage, Lord, to help change this situation.
You were a person who stood up for others,
and knew what it was like to be bullied.

Lord, help me to do my best for him,
and help us put an end to the bullying.

## *11* A QUARREL

Yesterday it was like love that would never end, Lord,
and today it's like all straw and ashes.

Why did I say what I said?
Why did I draw back and be dishonest,
when she asked me about someone else?
Can love change just like that?
Changing like sea which is rough one minute and calm the next?

My heart is like that now, Lord.
I still like her, still love her,
and feel upset and angry too.
Why can't she be more constant?
What's a joke one day is an insult the next.
And I suppose she's saying the same about me.

Help me, Lord.
Bring back the love.
Bring back the joy.

Sorry for dishonesty, for hurting.
But it didn't seem that serious to me.

I think we will get back again;
the old love will grow warm again.
I hope it will.

Maybe a good conversation,
clearing the air,
will deepen our love.
Lord, teach us both
what it means to love warmly and sincerely.

And give me hope that love is stronger than a quarrel,
and if this is real love, it will deepen and grow.
Give me courage, please Lord, to be honest and say what's in my heart.
Give me faith and trust in her, in myself,
and in your love through all this.

## *12* JEALOUSY

Lord, I hate that feeling,
the awful jealousy that comes over me,
and I hate it when others know that's how I'm feeling.
It gets me when someone
gets better than me at football and I hear him being praised,
or someone gets the limelight at a concert and she's on first.
Why do I feel like this?

Or the way I give out about people who do well in exams –
call them swots, accuse them of getting grinds,
when I know that the real problem is
I'm feeling jealous.

Why? I hate it,
it wrecks my day,
and wrecks good times with people.

Help me, Lord, when I feel like this;
I'm afraid of it,
scared it will take me over,
like a monster in my soul,
it's so strong.

I'm even jealous when my mother looks better than I do,
or my brother gets looked at by the popular girls,
or I just feel bad about myself.

Help me to see jealousy, Lord,
as more about me than about the other.
It's more that I feel bad about myself,
than that she's any better
or he's any stronger.

Help me, Lord, to accept myself
for what I am,
how I look,
how I think,
who my friends are.

Then I'll be happier.

Forgive me, Lord, when I lash out at the ones I'm
jealous of,
forgive me for my harsh words, judgements and even
the lies.

But more than forgive me, Lord, for I don't always
mean it;
heal me, strengthen me,
fill me with a certainty that you love me,
just as I am now.

## *13* LONELY

Lord, I feel lonely just now;
nobody around, house empty,
though sometimes that's nice,
just to play my own music, ring a friend –
but today it's different.
I felt left out when I wasn't asked to go bowling.
There's some tension between myself and him.
I feel I'm not as good as the others who go along,
and I wonder are they talking about me.
So I wasn't asked.
Why me?
Why wasn't he left out?

And I just feel rotten.
Can I not keep friends,
or do all my friendships turn to straw?

No one seems to care.
Others just laugh and say I'm too easily hurt.
But I feel it inside,
lonely, hurt, just as if I'm nobody.
Some people feel nearly suicidal when they feel so alone.

Do You care?

I feel I'm like an alarm clanging in a derelict building.
I'm derelict, friendless,
and is it always going to be like this?
And I'm like an empty clanging sound,
nobody hears.

Did you feel a bit like that
when You said to your friends,
'Can you not watch one hour with me?'

Help me, Lord,
to find good friends in life.
And when I feel so lonely,
help me to believe in myself,
and to know You as a friend,
who will always be near.
Thanks, Lord, for Your friendship,
especially when I'm lonely.

## *14* Bad at home

Lord, I find it hard in our family;
so much aggro, so much shouting,
it's as if we hate each other sometimes.
And there's also closeness and we care for each other;
but sometimes I wonder do I really care for them?

Still, I just want to get out of it.
And this makes me feel bad.

Lord, why do my parents shout so much at each other?
Did they make a bad mistake in marrying?
It's frightening, hearing them arguing,
and it spills over to us,
and we're all arguing with each other.
The younger ones are suffering from it,
they're scared even to be at home now.

Why can't our family be normal?
Can we not have meals without insults?
Or there's a silence you could cut with the knife.

And the drinking and the gambling,
the beatings and the hatred;
it's too much for me, I'm not old enough.
I want to enjoy being young
like my friends.
I want to be able to bring my friends home,
but I never know what the atmosphere will be like.

I feel like saying, try it all on someone else;
why am I in this family?
Do You care at all?
Help me to believe You really care for us,
at least that You care for me.
I feel at times that I'm too responsible.
I can't make things right for everyone,
I'm too young.

Help my parents, Lord.
Help me.
Give me the trust to know You are close to me,
I believe You are.

## *15* We can't talk to each other

It's hard to get it right at home, Lord.
I just can't talk to them,
any of them, even my brother.

I want to get away from them,
I can't stand it anymore.
But I'm too young yet,
and I need them.

Lord, help me.
I know I'm hurting them,
but I just lose the cool any time we get talking.

It's all about working hard or I won't get a job,
not going out and coming home early.
At times I know they're right,
and they're afraid for me,
that I'll get into drugs or fail exams.
I never say this, Lord,
but there is a lot I'm grateful for.
They have looked after me for a long time,
they're generous with money.
and they do love me.

But they just don't know how stupid I feel.
Will this problem ever go?
I'd like to get on better with them.

I'm starting to tell lies and then I feel dishonest
I'm jealous of my brother's better school work,
and that my sister is more popular with friends than I am.

I'm often afraid of life,
but I need some friends,
and I don't always like the people I hang out with.

Maybe I'll try to talk to them at home,
What can I do to get out of the mess?
If I hurt them, I find it hard to say sorry
and so do they.

Lord, look after them.
Help me not to hurt them more than I do.
Stop them hurting me.
Just get them to give me space,
give me a chance to grow up my way.

Just help me to be a bit more friendly.
Help me to make it work this time.

## *16* ALCOHOLISM AT HOME

I'm always asking why, Lord:
Why does Dad drink so much?

Today he's drunk again,
snoring in the chair downstairs,
and I dread when he'll waken up.

I don't know how he'll be:
will he scream at us
or want to buy something for us,
or be crying and hugging us all?
I don't know which is worse.

At times, Lord, I feel so angry.
Why does he do this to us?
He loves his drink more than he loves us.

I hate bringing people home.
I can't tell anyone about it.
I'm afraid for Mum.
She says so little about it;
but she's suffering too in her own silence.
Is she afraid of him?
I'm scared of their rows,
and especially when he shouts at her.
Lord, help him, help her, help us.

Help us, Lord.
I'm afraid of him,
will we run out of money,
will he run away on us,
will he die?

Sometimes I wish he'd go away.
And I hate myself for that.
Help me; help all of us.
Don't You love him too?
Help him give up the drink.

Let me find someone to talk to.
And don't let me hate you
because he's like that,
but that's how I feel sometimes –
why couldn't you have got me a father who doesn't
drink?

At least you don't think
there's something wrong with me,
because he drinks.
Thanks for your love,
for being part of the family;
I need your help now, Lord.

## *17* PREGNANCY

We made a mistake, Lord;
our sex was unplanned, a mistake,
and we're suffering for it.

We're expecting a child;
we didn't intend to have sex,
nor did we have it often.
Why us?

Others haven't paid like we have;
and they don't seem to try
to respect each other as we did.
It's frightening;
telling people –
parents, friends, teachers.

Will we have to leave school?
What will it be like for us
when everyone knows?
We want to stand by each other,
even when we're furious at each other,
blaming each other, blaming ourselves.
All I can ask, Lord,
is be with us.
It's not Your fault,
but it does seem harsh
that it happened to us.
We need love and understanding now;
and we're grateful for those who care.

Help us both, Lord.
Give us confidence in each other,
and in You.
Don't leave us in the dark
it can be very cold and lonely for us,
and we wonder is there any light,
or is there any peaceful music
in all the sounds of our heads.

Help us, Lord, You condemn nobody.
Help us not to condemn ourselves;
let us know You are near,
and calm our fears.

## *18* SECRETS

Lord, You know there are things I tell nobody,
secrets which I don't want others to know about:

what I hope for in my life,
what I want to be,
someone I love,
someone I fear,
what people have done to me,
people I'm angry at.

My secrets can bring me to life,
or can be depressing.

They can be feelings I have that I don't like,
or a family secret I'm ashamed of,
or abuse that happened in the past.
Maybe a relationship I'm ashamed of,
or a pregnancy I feared,
a robbery or some other dishonesty,
some guilt or anger I feel and don't share.
*...Name your secret as honestly as you can.*

Help me, Lord, please help me.
I'm like a shell blown along the beach,
with something inside I want nobody to see.
It's like having a diary hidden at home
and always fearing someone will find it and read it.

Lord, I want to hide, I need to hide,
like hiding away something stolen.

Or do I?
When I find a friend I can be open with,
or tell You about my secrets,

then I'm freer, happier, more myself.
Help me not to hide from You and from myself,
and help me find someone I can share secrets with.

At times I feel others do know;
they know what my secrets are.
And then I'm afraid, naked, vulnerable.

Do You know, Lord?

Of course You do, for You know me
through and through.
Please love my secrets;
if I know You love them, maybe I can love them too.

Did You have secrets, Lord?
You often told people not to say things about you.
Not to say that You knew You would be killed,
or that You were the Son of God.

My secrets aren't as big as that,
but to me they're big.

Here it is, Lord,
*...say out one secret to the Lord.*

You love me, Lord,
all of me, past, present and future.
Help me to love myself,
and to love, not fear,
the secrets of my heart.

## *19* Shadows

I like shadows on the road, Lord.
It was a quiet and warm evening,
and the sun put long shadows on the road.

I thought of the shadows of life,
times when the light seems dim,
like when I fail an exam,
or a friendship goes sour,
or I seem to mess up the family with my temper,
or I think of the fights at home,
or when I don't know what I'll do in the future.

In the shadow of failure,
let me know the light of hope,
and in the shadow of quarrels,
let me know the light of forgiveness.
For there's no shadow without some light,
like the shadows on the road
are caused by the sun or the moon.

In the shadows of a fall-out in friendship,
let me know the light of love,
that there can always be a making-up or new friends
round the corner.

In the shadows of rows at home,
let me know the light of compassion,
and let me know I can find security in many people,

and in Your love and care for me, Lord.
When I don't know what to do in the future,
give me patience and guidance;
I believe You have hopes for my life,
that I can do something really worthwhile for You.

Help me believe, find meaning
in all the darkness of life;
help me see darkness
as the beginnings of new light,
like your cross was the beginning of resurrection.
May I always believe in the light within all the shadows.

## *20* Sexual confusion

Sex confuses me, Lord.
All the different feelings.
What do they mean?
How can I know what's right or wrong?
How can I not get let down or let others down?

People say young years are very confusing for a while;
at our age sexual feelings are very strong,
and they are new and exciting.

I can get very strong attractions,
and I really want to get to know someone,
and I want to get close to someone,
and I want to express what I feel.
But I know there can be a lot of hurt,
when people use each other.

Can I be in love with two people at the same time?
What about feelings for my own sex,
and questions about being gay?
Or what about being attracted to an older person?
Or maybe everyone has questions like these?

And all the different messages
from school and home,
media and friends,
get me mixed up about what's good and bad,
right and wrong,
loving and just using someone else.

Lord, help me to control my sexual feelings;
I don't want them controlling me.
Help me to feel good about my sexuality,
for You created it as You created everything of me.
May my sexuality be a means of affirming another,
now and in the future.

For the ways I have failed to respect others and myself,
I ask Your forgiveness.
Heal my hurts and hurts I have caused.

Thanks for people who have cleared up some of this
confusion,
and for friends and older people who have helped me,
and thanks for Your gift of sexuality.

In all my hopes and desires to be a person of love,
be near me, Lord of warmth, affection and of love.

## *21* Inside a shell

That shell he goes into, Lord,
I can't understand it.
What goes on inside him?

The shell on the outside:
Her silence when the family want to do something she won't do – is it just wanting her own way?
His silence when someone doesn't like another of his friends – is it his insecurity?
Her silence when a friend goes off with someone else – is it jealousy?
Lectures from parents about drink when they drink themselves – what are they trying to hide?

I'm stuck.
What's going on inside?
A mask comes over the face,
a shell hides the feelings,
a small, thin wall of glass seems to separate us,
and the glass is almost transparent
but you can't see through it.
The shell is so fragile that it would smash
if I asked a question.
Is the mask more attractive to him
than what he believes is inside?

It's as if feelings and truth are put in a deep freeze.
What did You do, Lord, with
shells, masks, frozen moments

between people?
It seems that only love,
patient, gentle, kind love broke through.

That's hard,
because I have my own masks, shells and fears.
When he puts on a mask, I go into my shell,
or when she goes into her shell, I put on a mask.
And then the walls between us get thicker and higher.

If the friendship is not too important, I'll walk away.
But I want to get through the wall, inside the shell,
behind the mask to the real person.
Help me, Lord, help us,
when we want to deepen what's between us,
not to be afraid of
what's inside the shell,
behind the mask,
over the wall.
You are there, Lord.
You are inside the shells, masks and walls,
loving, caring, kind, for each of us.
Help us, Lord, to find You in our honesty.

## *22* ALWAYS A STORY

Why did my sister flare up at me today?
I only asked a simple request:
would she leave me to the bus?
It's a long walk and she has a car.

Lord, what was it?
I really got a blaze of her fury.

She told me later,
and now I know there is always a story.
A late night, a row with her boyfriend,
and a worry if her job will last.
I was just the occasion, not the cause, of the outburst.

When I know that,
it makes it easier to forgive, to get over the hurt.

## *23* EVERYONE HAS A STORY

Why does he sit in the class looking out the window,
never joining in?
Maybe his sister is in trouble or his brother is ill.
Why does she go shoplifting at the weekend?
Maybe she wants kicks in life and her family do it.
Why was she so happy today?
Maybe a new job or some other good news.
Why does he have to get drunk to enjoy himself?
Is he so insecure that he can't talk to us without drink?

I remember the time we had a row in class,
and found out the teacher's mother
was critical in hospital.
We felt small, humbled,
and realised that we all have a story,
and the story explains our behaviour.

Lord, help me always to believe
that there is a story and a reason
why someone judges harshly, misunderstands, flies off
the handle.
Help me to open my mind and heart and ask 'Why?'
May I never too easily think I understand someone,
especially those I'm closest to.
Lord, give me more of Your compassion,
for that's what it means to love.

## *24* Am I religious?

Even though I find the Church hard, Lord,
I think I'm a spiritual person.

Lord, I like to think about You and talk to You,
I like what You say in the gospel about life,
but I get steamed up when I go to the church.
Words I can't relate to,
people who don't seem to understand me
or my age-group,
or understand much of life as I see it lived.

Lots of talk about money,
unsympathetic sermons on things we find hard,
like breakdown in marriage, sex at our age, gay people,
and I wonder do I really belong there.

But I'm not switched off by what You say
about love and respect and sympathy;
You seem very compassionate and understanding,

and want to help the poor.
And I like reading bits of the gospel.
Am I too hard sometimes,
harder on others than I'd want them to be on me?
Am I believing everything in the papers
or what I hear on the radio
about what's wrong in the Church,
and not testing out if it's true.

And people who are public on their faith,
leaders in the Church,
people in the parish,
they turn me off with gossip, dishonesty, insincerity,
and with the public scandals of abuse and sex and
wealth.
But I don't want them to turn me off You.

Do You understand?
When I meet people who seem to understand,
then I think You do.

Help me to be sincere to my own faith
and open to the faith of others.
Help me to believe in the mystery of religion,
and to realise that I won't understand some of it.
And help me to find You
on my own unique journey of life.

## *25* Exam failure

Lord, I've failed my exam.
It's hard now to say this;
I know I feel bitter,
and I know I worked harder than some who passed.
Lord, did You ever fail an exam?
Does anyone really know what it's like?

Others wasted time when I was studying;
there were nights I stayed in to write up notes
when I could have gone to a disco.
Why have I failed?
Why didn't You give me more brains?
Questions, no answers.
I don't want to cry any more.
I've done all my crying.
Help me to move on now.

I don't want to be bitter,
to be jealous of others' success.
But it was hard to enjoy the night out,
when others were feeling better.

Thanks for the look across the room from a friend;
I think he understood and that helped.

Help me to believe what people say:
that a good effort is what matters,
that I'm not a failure – I've just failed an exam,
and that good will come out of it.

Have I let down my parents,
teachers,
others who helped me?

I can't feel all this now,
though I believe some of it.
And I know many people who got something good
out of their failure.

Right now, it's dark,
and it's like when there's no break in a traffic jam.
At least let me feel Your presence,
a hand in the dark,
a path in the forest, even if I can't feel confident.

Give me hope that I'll get back to myself,
and that failure will make a better,
stronger person of me,
and thanks for the people who cared today.

Above all, Lord, please help me
not to see myself as a failure;
let me be always confident that You believe in me.

## *26* Exams are over

I'm glad they're all over, Lord.
It's been a tough few weeks,
a lot of anxiety.
And I was tired a lot of the time.

Some of us fell out a bit as well,
it must have been the tension
that made us say things we're sorry for now.

Lord, I did the best I could.
I hope I get through well.

It's great to be finished,
like fresh air in a stuffy room,
like the sunshine breaking through a cloud,
a good feeling of getting through something tough.

Thanks for Your help during the exams;
I felt You were close to me,
even during the exams I found hard.

I hope I'll get the results I want.
Help me to be confident till the results come out.

Help all the class as well,
especially those who think they did badly.
Thanks for the friends we made in the class,
and bless them now and always.
And thanks for the teachers
who did their best to get us through,
especially those who gave us extra time
during the exams.
Thanks for my parents and family,
who gave me support in the exams
and looked after me.

Lord, give all of us
the confidence to know our own value
no matter what the results.
And I hope we can always use our talents,
our intelligence and our study
in Your service.

## *27* I HATE MY STUTTER

I hate my stutter, Lord;
why can't I talk like everyone else?
I feel different, silly,
I don't open my mouth to say anything
because I may not be able to.
Help me;
cure me.

It's like having a scar
and a person doesn't want to have a shower after a match,
in case others would see it and laugh.
Or being small and feeling everyone's talking about me.
These things make us feel bad about ourselves.
We want a cure, or to feel it's not the end.

Could anyone like me?
Want to go out with me?

Times when the stutter just takes over,
and I feel there's no more to me than this.

Help me know there's more to me
than how I speak
or how I look
or my family's problems.

I blame you,
but maybe causes like this are mysterious.
Why me, Lord?
Help me grow through the different problems of my life,
see what's good about me,
rejoice in all that's good,
and be grateful.

And maybe sometimes, I don't know when,
my stutter or scar or problem or illness
will mean that I can help someone else.

## *28* MISTAKES

Lord, I've made a mistake there
and I made it before.

It's like when I don't tell the truth,
drink too much,
gossip about someone I like,
try to cut corners for some study,
cut time on the job,
give something from the job to someone,
Lord, help me learn from my mistakes.

And some mistakes harm others also:
gossip, dishonesty,
and I ask your forgiveness.

I get tired of some mistakes,
because I make them again and again.
I feel foolish, and I wonder what people think.
Help me, Lord, to learn from my mistakes,
for the only lasting mistake
is the one I don't learn from.

Build me up, Lord,
and let me be encouraged
to leave the past behind,
with its mistakes,
and move with confidence
into the future.

## *29* THAT LAST DRINK

I didn't really want that last drink, Lord,
but I felt I had to take it.
Most of them were having another one.
I knew I had had enough already,
and that I was intending not to take more.
And then the last one led to another,
and I even had to borrow money for the last one.

It's the same story –
who runs my life for me?
Why can't I just say No?

I seem to need to be seen to be part of that group,
and I'd be lost without them.
I enjoy the fun,
I like them,
but I don't always feel I can be myself.
And do we always have to have a lot of drink to get on together?

I don't think I have a drink problem, Lord,
but I do have a problem with them.

I admire the others who don't take a drink at all,
and seem to get on okay,
probably even better.

Maybe if I respected myself more,
I'd not feel I had to please them all the time.

Lord, I know You love me.
And You understand why I do this.
I want to be well in.

Help me first to be well in with myself,
to respect who I am for myself,
and then their opinions won't be so important.

## *30* TALKED ABOUT

It really hurt, Lord, when I heard that back.
I thought he was a friend and could keep a confidence.
And not everything he said was true.

I trusted him to keep what I had said secret,
and I thought we had a good friendship.
I know I said a few things about another girl
that I shouldn't have said.
And I had told him a few things which were secret.

Why did he spill it all out?
Did it mean he got tired of me,
hated me?
Something good has gone from our friendship.

I don't want to trust him again.
If I tell him all this, I'm afraid he'll just laugh.
And I'm getting afraid to trust anyone.

It hurts, Lord, and I find it hard to forgive him.
Maybe later, not now.

Maybe the friendship wouldn't have lasted.
It was getting a bit dead anyway.
Help me not to be bitter,
help me to trust others in the future,
even though that's hard to do.
Help me some time to forgive him
as You have forgiven me.

Lord, let my anger sink into Your care;
let my hurt be healed,
and help me to know deeply
Your friendship and care.
And in that care and friendship
let me forgive, trust and love again.

## *31* SUICIDE

Lord, why?
That's the question all of us have.
We didn't know he was so unhappy.
Did he cover it over, was it going on long?
Did we miss signs that he felt messed up inside?

We need help, Lord,
from You or from someone,
just to come to terms and accept
that he is gone.

Could he not have asked for help,
told us why he was messed up?
Is that anger at him?
Probably.
Help us, Lord,
help me,
make sense of this,
help us understand his motives,
and help us forgive him when we blame him,
and in all our talk about him
help us love him more.

I feel guilty and upset.
I should have noticed.
Maybe we said things that hurt and we didn't know?
Give us the help we need, Lord,
not to be blaming ourselves.

Welcome him home, Lord, to Your place of rest.
Give him the peace he looked for and never found.
Help us to make something good out of all this.
Maybe we'll come closer to You through it,
though that's hard.
Help each of us to see
that suicide is not the solution
no matter how bad we feel.

Help his mother, his father, his family.
They must feel awful.
Let us feel thankful for the good times we had,
and value life and friendship and care.

Be with anyone who feels like he did,
with Your presence and friendship,
and send help in their path.

Give to all of us who miss him
the peace You now give him;
give us the strength to support each other,
and support especially those who miss him most.

And let our faith grow through this:
that You can help us through,
and that we can help each other through
this rough time
to a brighter time.

Let us remember him with love.

## *32* Young death

What's the meaning, Lord, of so young a death?
A young life, vivacious, optimistic,
ending in a short illness.

Her family is devastated, shocked, unbelieving at times.

Has love gone to death?
To nothing?
So much care given and received in a short time.

I don't like the phrase,
'since it has pleased You to call her home'.

Doesn't it call on all our reserves of trust?
That there is no waste of life,
that there is full and new life for her,
that all of us, her whole family,
can be enlivened and renewed,
made even stronger in our tragedy.
Love never ends, never dies.
We still love her, she loves us.
And love is the air of a wide, wide world;
it is the air we breathe into future love and friendships.
And I want to believe that
You welcome her home,
a young, loved woman going to her lasting home.

She gave us love,
and for this we are grateful,

and that is something
neither death nor life,
no illness, no sorrow
can take from us.

Lord, we miss her,
and are grateful for what she gave us.
May she share with us now
the life You share with her.

May her prayers and Your love, Lord,
ease our pain, soothe our mourning,
and comfort our sorrow.

### *33* A FRIEND'S DEATH

Why did he die?
That's all I was asking,
all during the funeral days.

Why?

His death made me sad, angry, fearful.
I liked him; I still do.
We enjoyed being with him,
he was a big part of the group I'm in;
I'll always have the memories.

Such a waste.
A wet night,

maybe too fast on the motor bike.
Seems such a waste now.
The injuries were huge
and nothing more could be done;
but we just didn't believe he would die.
I'll always remember those last few days.

Why?

Someone says if you want an answer to that question,
you'll be disappointed.

But it seems so cruel,
a life, a good life, snuffed out,
like a candle getting drowned in wax,
and the lovely flame is gone.
I'm afraid I'll forget,
that the memory of a good and lovely friendship will dim.

Lord, did You have to take him?
Did You not want to save him on the bike?

What does it mean that You love us?
Do You love me when I feel so angry at You,
angry at him for the death?
Just like when we feel angry
that people didn't take care of themselves?

I want some peace;
to feel again the friendship that was part of us.

I know this won't bring him back,
but I'm asking You to give me some peace.

You wept when Your friend died.
all I can feel is that You're weeping now.

Help me know the light of Your presence.
Console us all,
friends, even more so, the family.

I hope, Lord, that all we found together
will never die, but carry on
for the rest of our lives.

## *34* Trusting

I was about six
and got onto the bike;
a small bike, just for my size.
How would I balance?
A skill now second nature;
but the first half mile
was guided by my father's hand.

No learning without trusting,
and moving off when he let go.

Thanks for memories of trust.
The trust that I'd be collected from school;
the trust that parents' love would last, and I'd be safe;
the trust that love was the centre of the home.

Trust grows for all of us
from the earliest age.
And it grows or is damaged.

I'm angry that I wasn't let trust myself
when I was told not to sing in a class,
because I picked up much more than that I couldn't sing.
It meant I was different, I was not as good as others,
and that others could beat talent out of me.

I'm angry at boys who steal from the cloakroom in
school,

and at girls who pretend to like someone when going
with someone else.
And at people who abuse or try to abuse young bodies;
what they have done is more than a moment's crime,
they have broken our trust in people,
and breaking trust for another is one of the biggest
faults I know.

Thanks for the man who looked after me in a shop
when I got lost;
for the aunt who always remembered my birthday;
for the friend who told me I was okay as a small
fifteen-year-old
when size was so important –
it's not now, but the trust is.

Their gift was the light of trust,
or the pathway to guide me into life.

Lord Jesus, help me to trust;
heal the broken trust-places in my soul.
Thanks for those who gave me trust;
and thanks for Your faithful friendship to me.

Please, Lord, let me be the type of person
that others will trust.
I give them this gift.
In giving it to them, I give it to You.

## 35 Who imagines my life?

I'm caught, Lord;
so many pressures.
What I wear,
who I'll vote for,
attitudes to religion,
jobs I can get,
points in exams;
who is running my life?
I want to be able
to make my own decisions,
and live by values I believe in,
when I'm trying to be just and good.
And I think that's what You want.

I've spent money on tapes I don't really want,
I buy clothes and soaps I don't want either,
but friends and advertising just have loud voices,
and I feel tense inside.

Lord, help me to be my own person;
help me to become what I can become with You.

It's like as if someone is planning my life for me,
and I buy what they planned
or reject what they don't like.
Others seem to plan how I use
my money, my sexuality, my intelligence.
Do I have a say in my life's plans?
Lord, help me not to be drowned in others' expectations.

I imagine life – happy, loving, caring,
free to be good, to do good,
free to give my approval to what I really approve of,
able to reach for what I believe in myself.

Some of the pictures of Your life, Lord,
help me to imagine my own life.
Pictures of how You treat others,
especially people who are down:
with compassion, kindness,
not forcing them to You.
You invite people
to a really full life,
giving their talents for the gospel.

I see it in how You forgive people,
especially those close to you,
and in Your view of possessions and reputation,
that these are in the service of love.

I want to be drawn, Lord, by the pictures of Your life:
pictures of courage, forgiveness,
constancy and love.

Help me to live in Your dream for me,
Your plans and Your hopes.
Help me to believe these will bring me happiness.
You have come to bring life and bring it to the full.

## 36 DREAMS OF THE FUTURE

A lot of thoughts came back to me, Lord,
as I sat by the river where we used go as kids,
I remembered when we came here as kids,
I liked coming here and enjoyed it.

We came, all the family,
and it was a good time.
I was only five or six,
I loved them, they loved me,
and could feel the warmth and security.

That's what I still want;
times I look at the river and hope
I'll be able to to give and receive love in my life.

Help me to recover the dreams of a child,
when I wanted to love everyone,
and be loved by them;
when I wanted to be generous and give things away –
not everything but a lot!
When I wanted everyone to be happy, content
and united,
and when I liked flowers and birds and trees.

I don't want to get simple, Lord,
and think that this would cure all the world;
but some of these dreams are Your dreams,
and I'd love to live for them.

I've been hurt and I turn in on myself
and don't want to open my heart to love.
I've been rejected
and then I get cold and mean.
I've been laughed at and then I get afraid
and don't care about other people's happiness.
I've been let down
and then I'm afraid of closeness.

Lord, help me keep in touch with my dreams
for compassion, for love, for caring.
You give me these dreams,
and I know You're near,
when I want to live out of them and for them.

## *37* DECISION ABOUT THE FUTURE

Lord, help me,
as I go through the application forms;
planning study in the future,
looking for a job,
or getting on a training course,
wondering whether I'll be able for what I want,
if there are jobs in it,
or if I'll be happy in it.

It's a big moment;
thanks for it.
Thanks for the chances that have led me to school;
and even though I hate school sometimes,

I'm glad I have an education.

All the different voices when I'm choosing for the
future.

They tell me:
pick something you like,
pick something that you'll get into,
pick something you'll get a job out of.
I don't know.
I may make the wrong choice.
I may not get what I want.
I mightn't be able for it,
mightn't be happy.

I feel a lot of pressures;
my parents want the best for me
and they're worried.
Teachers give different advice,
and I wonder do any of them really know me.

I want to do something good,
worthwhile, fulfilling with my life.
as well as something I like,
something I'll get a job from,
something I'm into.

What I really want to do, I may not get into.
Help me, Lord, to make the right decision.
Help me to know also that it's one of many choices
I'll have to make in life.
Let me get what will make me happy,

what will give use to my talents.
And what do You want?
Have You any plan for me?

Don't let me be just selfish when I choose.
I want to do something which will make a difference
to my own life and will help others.
I want to make a difference in the world.
Help me to be aware of what brings me peace in Your presence,
and gives me some sort of harmony in my heart.

Lord, I offer these thoughts to you;
through my decision I want to do the best
for myself and for You,
for my future family if I marry,
for the people I live among;
help me to bring the gospel into my decision,
and to be a person for others.

## *38* INTO THE FUTURE

Lord, I often wonder
about the future
and what it will be like for me.
I see people a few years older –
some of them frighten me,
others give me a bit of hope.

Will I get through exams?
Will I get a job?

Will I be happy?
Will I keep friends?
Who will I marry
and will it work out?

Or I wonder about myself.
What do people think of me?
I think I get on okay with my friends –
some of the time –
but sometimes I'd like to know for definite.

And I wonder about You.
What are You like?
I think You're a good friend,
You seem to understand me,
want the best out of me,
want the best for me,
but don't seem to ask more than I can be.

Did you feel like I feel –
excited at life sometimes,
ashamed other times of who I am,
confused but full of love.

When I wonder with joy, I'm grateful to you;
when I wonder with fear, I want Your help.
Let me know You're beside me, when I let my mind wander,
and I daydream about the future,
and what I'll be like.

Daydream in me, Lord!
Let my dreams for myself be
worthy of all who love me,
be worthy of me,
be worthy of You.

## *39* DESIRE TO LOVE

I feel a great desire in me, Lord,
to love someone totally
and be loved in return.
This is what I want in my life.
I think of it often, daydream about it,
and think of my children in the future.

Who will I marry?
Strange to think there is someone
whom I might not have yet met,
whom I will marry.

To someone now unknown, except to You,
I will promise life and love forever.

I'd like that:
there's something great about giving totally
  to someone else,
and receiving totally,
and having children,
and wanting to give them everything of myself.
Help me Lord, now,

to live so that I can be a good partner,
faithful, caring, open to another special person.
Help me to grow in being unselfish.

Please, Lord, let me know Your love for me,
and then I have some idea of what love forever
will be like.
Thanks for the desire to marry, to be a parent.
It's great to think that Your big command –
love one another as I have loved you –
is also what I want most in life.

## *40* I WANT TO GIVE

There are times, Lord,
when I really want to make a difference in the world.
I admire people who seem taken up
in something bigger than themselves.
When I die I want people to be able to thank me for something –
is that selfish?

No.
You said, 'remember me'.
You want people to remember You every day.

You have given me talents which I like
*...mention some of your good qualities...*
I want to enjoy them and give them to You:

a good singing voice,
sports and art,
a sense of humour.

Or talents like being able to listen,
to be sympathetic,
to get into a friend's world and help.
These talents,
and I'm shy to mention them to others,
are part of what I want to offer in my life:

to my friends,
the family at home,
the person I'll marry,
the children I hope to have,
the neighbourhood I will live in.

Lord, give me a generous spirit,
a kind heart,
a courageous soul,
an energetic body,
so that some of what You have given me
will reach others.

## *41* Mountain prayer

I enjoyed the day in the mountains, Lord.
Seemed we were in the middle of Your creation,
surrounded by Your peace and refreshment.

The air was fresh,
sounds were clear as a bell,
it was like being at the beginning of something.
Even though these mountains
have been there for centuries,
it seemed as if they were all just new that day.

Is that what You are like, Lord,
always new, never ageing?
And we're like that too,
even though we look the same
we're new, strong, part of You.

Thanks, Lord, for creation:
for the strength of the mountains,
the pathways leading to the top,
the streams, the trees, the flowers,
the animals we saw – a deer in the distance;
thanks for beauty and freshness and creation,
the beauty unites us in a good feeling together.

The mountains are strong like You, Lord.
And You are always making them.
It's not that You made them years ago
and now sit somewhere just watching them.

Your life keeps them strong and lovely.
You're always growing new trees,
putting down deeper roots,
giving fresh water to streams;
that's the way You make everything,
and You are all the time making us.

Help me Lord, to know that You are always involved in
my growing-up,
Your love grows me, makes me bigger, stronger, more
alive,
and Your love is the sure pathway of my life.
Please, Lord, let me be thankful for all You make,
and that You're making the best of me all the time,
day by day, a loving glance each moment.

For this making of me, thank You, Lord.

## *42* Music

I like that song, Lord;
it cheers me up,
gets me out of myself,
reminds me of some good friends.

Thanks for music, songs,
for times we sang together.
At a party,
at the beach,
in the school,
in the choir, the folk group;
music is one of Your gifts.

Thanks for those who have a great voice,
and for the lift to the heart and soul they bring.

The band brought us together;
I hope they're all okay now.
Look after.......who left the band,
and we haven't heard of her since.
Thanks too, Lord,
for the times when music helped us.
At the funeral,
at the wedding,
when we were finishing school.

Times when words were few
and we didn't know what to say.

Help me, Lord, to appreciate music.
Sorry for the ways we misuse it.
May we always know it is one of the ways
that people spoke of You:
the song of God,
the silent music,
the harmony of the world.

Thanks, Lord, for the music I like.

## *43* THE SEA

Lord, when I look at the sea,
I think of depths and storms and calm.

The sea has so many moods:
calm like a chat with a good friend,
turbulent like a quarrel in love,
rough like an argument in friendship,
and it speaks to my different moods.
I love being by the sea, Lord;
I love to sit by it, walk by it, run into it.

The water calls for trust
in life and people and in You, Lord,
it calls on me to trust
in You, in myself and in others.

In the depths of the sea is Your power,
and in the depths of myself is Your creation.
Help me, Lord, to trust,
to trust myself to the future
like a fish trusts itself to the depths of the ocean.

Help me to trust,
that life will be kind and its troubles will not overwhelm
me,
that people will be there for me on all of life's paths,
that I'll be able to say yes to a person or a commitment
and make a choice to love and do good with my life.

Help me to trust in You,
that You are never far away,
that Your love never fails no matter what I do.

Help me to trust in myself,
that I am good, courageous and can live up to my choices.

Often I am afraid:
of people, of commitments, of failure,
of life not working out.
Into Your hands I put my hand, Lord;
lead me as You know best,
because You love me.

In fear give me trust,
in my insecurity, give me courage,
and always, give me Your love.